Your Guide to Government

What is the executive branch?

James Bow

PRESIDENT OF THE UNITED STATES

E PLURIBUS UNUM

Crabtree Publishing Company
www.crabtreebooks.com

Crabtree Publishing Company

www.crabtreebooks.com

Author: James Bow
Coordinating editor: Kathy Middleton
Series editor: Valerie J. Weber
Editors: Valerie J. Weber, Lynn Peppas, Crystal Sikkens
Proofreaders: Diksha Chopra, Kelly McNiven
Discussion questions: Reagan Miller
Production coordinator: Ken Wright
Prepress technician: Ken Wright
Project manager: Summit Kumar (Q2A Bill Smith)
Art direction: Joita Das (Q2A Bill Smith)
Cover design: Samara Parent
Design: Roshan (Q2A Bill Smith)
Photo research: Ranjana Batra (Q2A Bill Smith)
Print coordinator: Katherine Berti

Written, developed, and produced by Q2A Bill Smith

Photographs:
Cover: Shutterstock; Title page: Shutterstock; P4: Kamil
Macniak/Shutterstoc; P5: Universal Images Group Editorial/Getty Images;
P6: Paul J. Richards/AFP/Getty Images; P7: U.S. Navy/Handout/Getty
Images; P8: Jamie Squire/Getty Images Sport/Getty Images; P9: Mark
Wilson/Getty Images News/Getty Images; P10: Mark Wilson/Getty Images
News/Getty Images; P11: Cecil W. Stoughton/White House Press Office
(WHPO); P12: Darren McCollester/Stringer/Getty Images News/Getty
Images; P13: mediaphotos/iStockphoto; P14: Mesut Dogan/Shutterstock;
P15: Alex Wong/Getty Images News/Getty Images; P17: Spencer
Platt/Getty Images News/Getty Images; P18: David McNew/Getty Images
News/Getty Images; P19: Alex Wong/Getty Images News/Getty Images;
P20: Uwe Steffens/Picture Press/Getty Images; P21: The White House;
P22: Joe Raedle/Getty Images News/Getty Images; P23: Emmanuel
Dunand/AFP/Getty Images; P24: Justin Sullivan/Getty Images News/Getty
Images; P25: Tony Anderson/Taxi/Getty Images; P26: Jim West/Alamy;
P27: NASA; P28: Kevork Djansezian/Getty Images News/Getty Images;
P29: Johnny Habell/Shutterstock; P30: Danny Martindale/WireImage/
Getty Images; P31: Specialist 2nd Class Jesse B. Awalt/U.S.

Library and Archives Canada Cataloguing in Publication

Bow, James, 1972-
        What is the executive branch? / James Bow.

 (Your guide to government)
Includes index.
Issued also in electronic formats.
ISBN 978-0-7787-0902-2 (bound).--ISBN 978-0-7787-0907-7 (pbk.)

        1. Presidents--United States--Juvenile literature. 2. Executive
departments--United States--Juvenile literature. 3. Executive
power--United States--Juvenile literature. I. Title. II. Series: Your
guide to government

JK517.B69 2013   j352.230973   C2013-900355-X

Library of Congress Cataloging-in-Publication Data

CIP available at the Library of Congress

Crabtree Publishing Company

Printed in the U.S.A./092014/CG20140808

www.crabtreebooks.com   1-800-387-7650

Published in Canada
Crabtree Publishing
616 Welland Ave.
St. Catharines, ON
L2M 5V6

Published in the United States
Crabtree Publishing
PMB 59051
350 Fifth Avenue, 59th Floor
New York, New York 10118

Published in the United Kingdom
Crabtree Publishing
Maritime House
Basin Road North, Hove
BN41 1WR

Published in Australia
Crabtree Publishing
3 Charles Street
Coburg North
VIC 3058

Contents

The Three Branches

The government has a lot to do with your life. The government builds the sidewalks you walk on. It brings you clean running water. It helps pay for your schools.

Firefighters save lives and buildings. They work for the government. The police work for the government, too. The people who pick up trash also work for the government. Your taxes pay for all their jobs.

The U.S. government is sometimes called the U.S. federal government. It is split into three parts. Congress is the legislative branch. It makes the laws. The U.S. Congress is known as a bicameral legislature. This means it is divided into two houses, the lower house called the House of Representatives and the upper house known as the Senate. Members in both houses are chosen by voters in an **election**.

The president lives in the White House in Washington, D.C.

The judicial branch is made up of judges and courts. The Supreme Court is the highest court. They review the laws and decide the meaning of the **Constitution**. The judges are not elected by voters. They are **appointed** by the president and the Senate confirms his choices.

The president leads the **executive** branch. It puts the laws to work. The president and the people of the executive branch run the government. Millions of Americans work for the U.S. government, and the U.S. government works for you.

Barack Obama is the 44th president of the United States.

WHAT DO YOU THINK?

What kinds of jobs do government workers have?

5

The Executive Branch

More than 3 million people work for the executive branch of the government. Another 1,470,000 serve in the U.S. military. These workers serve the people of the United States and keep you and your family safe and healthy.

We choose a president and vice president to run the executive branch of the government. The president is the leader of this branch. He or she chooses or appoints other members to help enforce the laws made by Congress. The vice president helps the president and is able to take over if the president cannot complete his or her term.

The president picks members to be part of his cabinet, or group of **advisers**. These members are the heads of different parts of the government known as departments.

The Oval Office in the White House is the official office of the president.

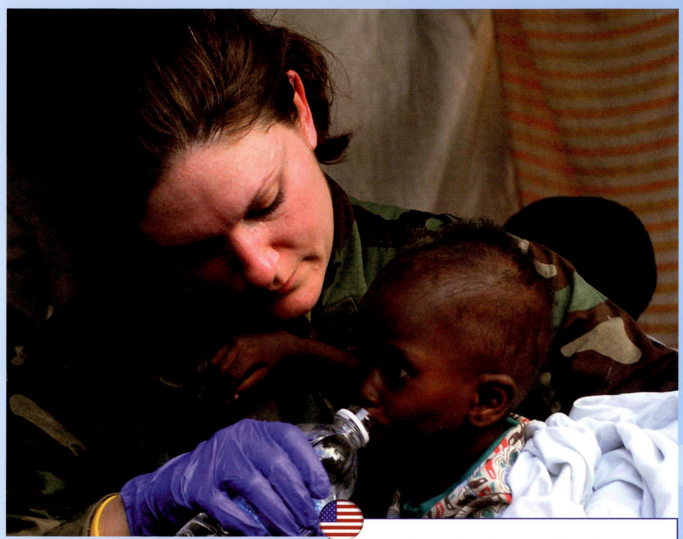

The U.S. Navy, like the rest of the military, is part of the executive branch. Sometimes the military helps care for people in other countries.

The departments each have a job to do, such as run the military, build roads, or make sure people obey the law. The heads of the departments are known as **secretaries**.

The Executive Office of the President, or EOP, is another part of the executive branch. These members work closely with the president. They help with decision-making or speaking to Americans on **behalf** of the president.

WHAT DO YOU THINK?

Who appoints the secretaries in the executive branch of government?

The President

Every four years we pick a president in an election to run our government. According to the Constitution, a president must be at least 35 years of age, be born in the United States, and have lived here for at least 14 years. Once the president has served a four-year term, he or she must then run for re-election. A president cannot be elected to office for more than two terms.

Congress passes **bills**. But bills become law only if the president approves them. Sometimes the president thinks Congress has passed a bad bill. Then he or she can refuse to approve it. The bill is then sent back to Congress for changes.

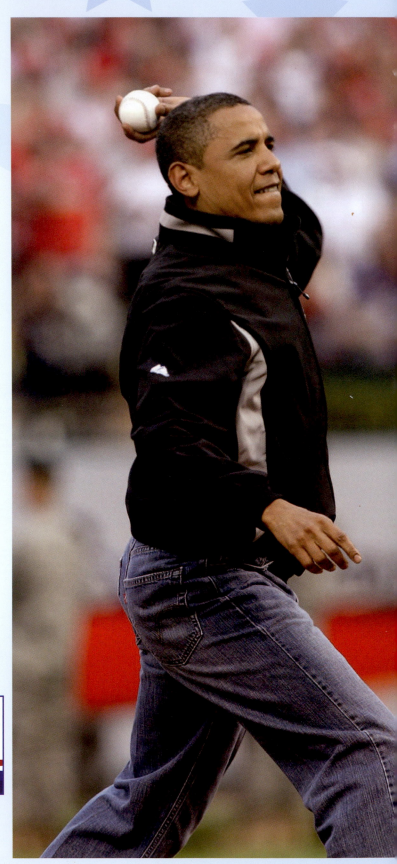

The president throws the first pitch of the baseball season. Sometimes this is part of the president's job.

The president is also the commander in chief. This title means the president leads the U.S. military. Generals and **admirals** report to the president, but only Congress can declare war.

The president picks judges for the Supreme Court. The Supreme Court is the most powerful court in our country. The president also picks the secretaries to run government departments. The president's choices for the judges and secretaries have to be approved by the Senate. The president has a say in all the people who run the government.

In 2008, President Obama picked Hillary Clinton to be his secretary of state.

In Their Own Words

"The executive Power shall be vested in a President of the United States of America."
The U.S. Constitution, Article II

The Vice President

The vice president runs with the president in an election. Both are elected together as a team. The vice president is second-in-command. This means the vice president's main job is to take over for the president if he or she cannot complete their term.

Nine vice presidents became president this way. In 1963, President John F. Kennedy was murdered. Vice President Lyndon Johnson became president that day. A president does not have to die to be replaced. In 1974, President Richard Nixon quit. Vice President Gerald Ford replaced him.

The vice president often steps in when the president is too busy. Here, Vice President Joe Biden gives a speech.

Vice President Lyndon Johnston promises to be president after the death of President John F. Kennedy.

The vice president is also the head of the U.S. Senate. Another senator, however, takes care of the daily work of leading the Senate. The vice president will often sit in on Senate meetings. Sometimes there is a tie when a bill is being voted on. The vice president breaks the tie. He or she decides whether a bill passes or fails.

The vice president often stands in for the president. He or she makes speeches and works to make sure the president gets the support of his or her **political party**.

WHAT DO YOU THINK?

Is being the vice president a powerful position? Why or why not?

The Cabinet

The president and vice president cannot run the country on their own. The job is just too big. So the executive branch is broken into parts. Each part has a job to do. One part runs the post office. Another part prepares for war. These parts are called departments.

There are 15 different departments. The president picks people to run these departments. They advise the president about how to run the country. They also pick other people to help run these departments.

The Department of Transportation watches over the railroads in the United States.

The Senate has to approve the president's choices for department heads. Once approved, these people become members of the president's cabinet and take the title of secretary, except for the head of the Department of Justice. He or she is named the attorney general. The secretaries serve as long as the president wants them to. The president can fire them or put them in another job for any reason.

The Department of Health and Human Services runs the Centers for Disease Control and Prevention. It helps keep deadly diseases out of the United States.

WHAT DO YOU THINK?

How many members are there in the president's cabinet?

EOP

The Executive Office of the President, or EOP, was created in 1939 to give the president help with all his duties and keep the executive branch running smoothly.

The number of people that are part of the EOP depends on the needs of the president. Today, there are over 1,800 people working for the EOP.

The president lives and works in the White House in Washington, D.C. The president's closest adviser is the White House chief of staff. The chief of staff **oversees** the EOP. He or she decides who can meet with the president, gathers reports from assistants, and gives the president advice. The press secretary talks to the **media** and gives updates on the president's schedule and activities.

In 2012, President Obama chose Jacob Lew to be the White House chief of staff. Lew is in charge of the people who help the president in the White House.

The Office of the Vice President, the Office of Management and Budget, and the National Security Council are all found in the Eisenhower Executive Office Building.

The staff that work closely with the president work from the White House. Other staff members work from the Eisenhower Executive Office Building across the street from the White House.

Protecting America

A big job of the U.S. government is to keep Americans safe. Two departments are in charge of this work. They are the Department of Defense and the Department of Homeland Security.

The Department of Defense runs the U.S. Army, Navy, Air Force, and Marines. Imagine that **terrorists** grab people from their home or work. The Department of Defense sends soldiers to save them. If pirates attack ships, it sends out the navy to catch them. If the United States has to go to war, the Department of Defense plans how to fight.

Homeland Security agents protect the country from terrorist attacks. Agents guard **border crossings** and **ports**. They check people coming into the United States. They look at goods entering the country as well.

These agents talk to people going through airports or crossing borders. They ask where the people are going and what they are bringing with them. The agents make sure people who would attack Americans do not enter the country. These agents keep airports and other public places safe.

Homeland Security also shares information about terrorists with law agencies like the Federal Bureau of Investigation (FBI), or spy agencies like the Central Intelligence Agency (CIA). They assist local police and work with the Department of Defense. This way, they help stop terrorists from attacking the country.

The Federal Emergency Management Agency (FEMA) is also part of Homeland Security. In the event of a natural or human-made disaster within the country, FEMA provides support and care for Americans.

The Department of Homeland Security was created after the September 11, 2001, terrorist attacks.

Keeping Americans Safe

More than 3.2 million people work for the Department of Defense. This number includes soldiers on U.S. bases and across the world. It also includes sailors on ships at sea. Other people fix the ships, tanks, planes, and other equipment used to fight. They, too, work for this department. The Department of Defense is the biggest employer in the world.

The Department of Homeland Security is smaller. It has just 200,000 workers. But their job is no less important. Both departments protect Americans from threats from inside and outside the country.

Homeland security agents work in airports. They make sure people have the correct papers to enter the country.

The Secretary of Defense Leon Panetta (left) sits next to the chairman of the Joint Chiefs of Staff General Martin Dempsey. As a member of the military, the chairman often advises the secretary of defense.

WHAT DO YOU THINK?

How are the Departments of Defense and Homeland Security different? How are they the same?

The State Department

The president often talks to leaders of other countries. He or she is speaking for the nation. But the president is not the only person who speaks for the country. The State Department also works with the governments of other countries.

The secretary of state talks to the leaders of other countries about problems. Sometimes the secretary makes promises or gives warnings. These dealings are called diplomacy. The president supports the secretary of state's dealings.

The Harry Truman Building in Washington, D.C., is the headquarters of the State Department.

President Obama and the prime minister of India meet in a state visit. The State Department helps the leaders of nations work together.

The State Department also runs embassies around the world. Embassies are government offices set up by one country in another country. Imagine you are in another country. Someone has stolen the papers allowing you to travel. You could go to a U.S. embassy to get help.

Or, imagine you get in trouble with the law in another country. The State Department makes sure you are treated fairly. The State Department also warns Americans which countries are not safe to travel to.

Enforcing the Laws

The government only works if the people follow the law. It only works if people pay for it, too. The Department of Justice makes sure people know what the laws are. It punishes those who do not follow the laws. The Treasury Department makes sure the government can pay for the things it does.

The attorney general leads the Justice Department. It is in charge of federal, or national, police agencies like the FBI. It also runs federal prisons.

The Secretary of the Treasury leads the Treasury Department. The Treasury collects taxes. Tax is the money you must give to the government. Taxes pay for all the people working for the government. The Treasury also prints the money that Americans spend. It makes coins and it even prints postage stamps.

The Treasury Department runs the U.S. Mint. The Mint prints America's money.

The FBI looks for evidence and catches people who break the law.

Like the Justice Department, the Treasury makes sure that laws are followed. They look for people who do not pay their taxes. People who do not pay their taxes sometimes go to jail. The Treasury also makes sure banks work within the law.

In Their Own Words

"... in this world nothing can be said to be certain, except death and taxes." Benjamin Franklin, one of the Founding Fathers of the United States, 1789

Hands-on Work

The president picks a cabinet. But the job of running the country does not end with them. Many other people work for the government. The public needs services from the government. These people provide those services. These men and women are part of the civil service.

The job of the civil service is to serve the public. Imagine you are getting a driver's license. The civil service includes the clerk who takes your picture and information as well as the person that gives you your driver's test.

The U.S. Post Office makes sure you get your mail.

Civil service also includes the rangers who patrol **national parks**. These civil servants watch campers and help them stay safe. There are more than 3 million people that work in various positions for the federal government in the United States. More than 300 thousand of them work in or near Washington, D.C.

Rangers sometimes give tours of national parks. They answer visitors' questions.

Helping the Government

Census workers count people across the United States. The census helps our government work better for the country.

The civil service does more than serve people directly. Government workers also do research. They gather information for the government to do its job properly.

Every ten years, government workers count how many Americans live in the United States and where they are living. They ask how much money each person makes and find out about the type of places people are living in. This process is called a census.

The census helps the government serve the public better. States that have grown in population get more positions in Congress. States that have fewer people get fewer positions. Areas that have more children may get more money for schools. The government also learns how to run its programs better. It learns if its laws are helping the country.

The government also supports science. NASA, or the National Aeronautics and Space Administration, was set up to explore space. It sent a robot to find out more about Mars. The research that NASA does teaches us a lot about outer space. It also helps us learn about our planet.

This rocket carried NASA instruments to search for life on Mars.

WHAT DO YOU THINK?

How often does the census take place? How does it help the government serve Americans?

The Government at Home

The executive branch exists to serve Americans. In the same way, state and city governments help Americans. Their services are often more direct.

City council meetings are a chance for people to speak out. They tell elected officials how they would like the government to run.

In Their Own Words

"The powers not **delegated** to the United States by the Constitution . . . are reserved to the States . . . or to the people."
Tenth Amendment to the U.S. Constitution

Without city firefighters, people would have to save their own buildings from fires.

State governments are run the same way as the U.S. federal government. A state's governor is like a president. Most states have a house of representatives and a senate. Every state has its own supreme court. State governments run state colleges. They build highways and hospitals.

Local, or city, governments are usually run by a council. Their leader is a mayor. Local governments build city roads and pipelines. They bring clean water into homes. City police keep the streets safe from crime. City workers pick up garbage and keep the streets clean.

Sometimes the work of the U.S. federal, state, and local governments are the same. The U.S. federal government has its own police. It also pays for schools and works to provide clean water. States and cities focus on their own people. The federal government works for all Americans. It is the U.S. federal government that fights wars, not the states.

Other Governments

Many other countries also have an executive branch in their government. In the United Kingdom, a queen or king is the **head of state**. Like the president, they sign all bills into law. In Canada and Australia, the governor-general is the head of state. But these heads of state do not have the powers that the president does. They are not elected. In these countries, the leaders of the legislative branch have more power. Many other countries have presidents, like France and Ireland. Some have more power than others. If the country is democratic, the president is elected to office.

Queen Elizabeth II is somewhat like Britain's president. She signs bills into law. She is not elected nor is she as powerful as a U.S. president.

Some presidents are not elected fairly. Robert Mugabe of Zimbabwe uses his army to stay in power.

DISCUSSION QUESTIONS

1. What three qualities do you feel are most important for a president to possess? Why do you think these qualities matter most?
2. Why is it important for the president to have a strong cabinet?

3. How can young people actively participate in the government? Brainstorm a list of meaningful ways young citizens can get involved.

Learning More

Books

Bedesky, Baron. *What Are the Levels of Government?* Crabtree Publishing, 2009.

Landau, Elaine. *The President, Vice President, and Cabinet: A Look at the Executive Branch.* Lerner Publications, 2012.

Websites

Ben's Guide to U.S. Government for Kids: bensguide.gpo.gov/3-5/government/branches.html

Congress for Kids—The Executive Branch: www.congressforkids.net/Executivebranch_index.htm

U.S. Government for Kids—The Executive Branch: www.ducksters.com/history/us_executive_branch.php

Glossary

admiral The leader of a navy

advisers People who give suggestions based on knowledge

appoint To select a person for a position or duty

behalf A representative for someone else

bills Plans for laws suggested by Congress but not yet approved by the president

border crossings Places where people and goods enter or leave a country

Constitution A group of laws that tell the U.S. government how it is to be run

delegated Given to

election The act of choosing by voting

executive Describes someone with the power to put laws into effect

head of state The person who leads a country

media Sources of information or news

national parks Scenic parks preserved and protected by the government

oversee To watch over or be in control of

political party A group of people that share the same views on how a country should be run

port A place where boats and ships dock

secretaries People hired to help the person in charge

terrorists People who kill other people to make a political point

Index